FIVE

Smooth

STONES

"ONE FATHER'S JOURNEY TO DEPOSIT
AND DEVELOP EXCELLENCE IN HIS
FIVE SONS"

R. V. SYKES, SR.

*"Then he took his staff in his hand, chose **five smooth stones**
from the stream, put them in the pouch of his shepherd's bag
and, with his sling in his hand, approached the Philistine."*
1 Samuel 17:40

To:
Randy
Anderson & Family

From:
R.V. Septich

Thanks for your support
and friendship
I Hope You Enjoy
Reading our
my 1st Book.

R.V. Septich

Dec 9, 2019

BOOK SUMMARY

Five Smooth Stones is about one father's journey
to deposit and develop
excellence in his five sons.

(Blessed Thanks)

Ablessed thanks to the love of my life, Christine Sykes; for without you none of this would have been possible. Thanks for your patience, understanding, encouragement, support, prayers and for not giving up on our dreams. No woman can ever compare to you. The countless sacrifices that you have made will forever be treasured by me. Thanks to my courageous sons Rick, Julian, Christian, Jalen and Caleb Sykes; for allowing me to share some of their personal stories. A blessed thanks to my loving and supportive mother, Dortha Mae Sykes. No matter what we've been through, you always demonstrated motherly love to all of us. Thanks to my father-in-law, Sylvester Johnson and my mother-in-law, Maggie Johnson, who welcomed me into the family and treated me like a son. Thanks to my brother-in-law (Greg Johnson) and my sisters-in-laws (Diane, Benita and Elizabeth Johnson) for accepting me into your family. We had our share of confrontations, but at the end of the day, we're family.

A very special thanks to my one and only daughter, Kourtney R. Sykes. Before I decided to write this book about fathering and mentoring five strong sons, I first had to obtain permission from her. I knew that she would be fine with my decision to write a book about the subject, but I did not want to take it for granted that my daughter would understand my reasoning for writing this book without including her. Thank you, Ms. Kourtney R. Sykes, my baby girl.

Special thanks to Belinda Gunn. I will always cherish your love, loyalty and listening heart. Special thanks to Mr. Eddie and Mrs. Gwen Blaine and the entire Prevailing Church Family for challenging and pushing me towards excellence. Thanks to our daughter in the faith, Angel Francis, for your love and support. Thanks to my granddaughter, Karis Peyton Sykes, for bringing more joy into the Sykes family. Thanks to my daughter-in-love for taking Julian off our hands. A blessed thanks to my best friends, Ron and LaShun Franklin, for being there for my family during one of the most difficult periods in our lives. To my brothers (Kenneth, Anthony, Demetrious and Ebony) Sykes; and cousins (Clayton, Troy and Gregory Mack). There has never been a dull moment when we're together; crackin on each other. Thanks to my cousin, Lamonica E. Sykes; your physical condition made all of us strong. Last, but not least, a blessed thank you to Mrs. Robin Thorpe for encouraging, challenging and pushing me to complete the book. Whether it was through Facebook, text, or just a phone call, you challenged me to get it done.

Thanks for being my first editor-in-chief and for working with me through this tedious journey. I can't wait to be involved with your first book.

(Special Acknowledgments)

Professor Diane M. Lockett, #1 Best-Selling co-author of the book, Mission Unstoppable: Extraordinary Stories of Failure's Blessings (with George Fraser and Les Brown). Thank you for reading my book and for putting the finishing touches on it. Your insight, professionalism, experience and words of encouragement truly blessed me.

(Dedication)

I would like to dedicate this book to the memory of my grandmother, Lois Dandridge, and my aunt, Martha Ann Sykes. Words cannot express what you meant to all of us. It seems as though both of you were right by our sides during those dark and difficult days. Grandma, there never was a time when I came to your house and you didn't have something on the stove. To my friend and brother, Calvin Gunn, who told me the truth, encouraged me and believed in me. There were times when you told me things that I did not want to hear; but because of your proven love for me, I received it. To my late and best friend back in the day, Frank Lambert.

Where Are They Now?
A Message to the Single Mothers
Acknowledgements to All the Men who were Instrumental
in My Life

Table of Contents

CHAPTER 1

(Summary Of Life)

"For I know the plans I have for you," declares the LORD,
"plans to prosper you and not to harm you, plans to give
you hope and a future"
Jeremiah 29:1

I was born 4 months after the 1967 Detroit Riots. So, it means that my mother carried me in her womb during one of the most difficult times in Detroit's history. Can anything good come out of Detroit? My mother gave birth to five sons. I am the third. I truly love and appreciate my mother, Dortha Mae Sykes, who did her best in trying to provide for us. We had some difficult times, but I thank God for my mother's love, support and the sacrifices that she made for all of us.

My mother, a single mom, did her best in trying to raise five boys in the inner city of Detroit. With the help of my grandparents and my aunt, we were (for the most part) kept in line and in order. We were all loved, disciplined (at times) and taught to respect adults, our neighbors and each other. My mother, grandmother and my aunt had no problem with getting the belt, switch or the closet thing they could put their hands on to get their points across.

In an effort to relieve my mother of the tremendous task of raising five boys, my two older brothers went to live with my grandparents. As a child, I could never understand why my older brothers lived separately from us. I knew that my grandparents loved all of us, but there were times when I felt my older brothers were their favorites. It didn't bother me. I just felt that way.

Although my younger brothers and I had different fathers, I can honestly say that my mother did not treat us differently. She never compared one father to the other or showed favoritism. In fact, she did not tolerate us comparing our fathers to each other. When we would argue about whose father is the best, how much money they had, what they bought us, how often we saw them and so forth, my mother would stop us dead in our tracks. She did not play that! My brothers knew how to get back at me. All they had to say to me was, "*at least my father isn't a criminal*". Just hearing those words would cause me to fly off the handle and retaliate against them physically.

My mother made it clear that we were not to engage in any type of negative conversation regarding our fathers. In fact, I don't ever recall hearing my mother talking negatively about either of our fathers. She did her best when trying to make sure that we were unified and that we respected each other. Fighting each other was a no-no in our home. That was an automatic "beat-down" regardless of who started it.

If there was one thing that I hated the most while growing up, it was seeing my mother physically, emotionally and verbally abused by her long-time boyfriend. There were days when I would see my mother's battered and bruised face. Anger, hatred and hurt would permeate my very being. My younger brothers and I would often talk about doing something to my mother's boyfriend, but for some reason we never carried it out. Other than my oldest brother, who did not live with us, I tend to think that if anybody would have eventually done some harm to him, it would have probably been me. As we got older, the abuse just stopped.

The more we moved and the further we moved away from my grandparents, the more disconnected I became. The more disconnected I became, the more freedom I had. The more freedom I had, the more I found myself gradually getting caught up in a web of destruction. Too much freedom, along with the lack of discipline, is a recipe for disaster. Having too much freedom would become my own worst enemy. I can honestly say that I was never disrespectful to my mother, nor did I talk back to her. I knew that if I did, she would have probably tried to severely injure or for that matter kill me.

I remember coming home after hanging out all day in the streets. My mother instructed my brothers to tell me to stay at home for the evening and not to go anywhere for the rest of

21

the day. They related the message, but I disobeyed. I allowed my friends to pressure me into disregarding what my mother's instructions were. And so, I left the house and headed to a party that we had heard about. I remembered leaving the house in the evening and did not return from that party until after 2 in the morning (at the earliest). As my friends and I walked home from the party, I saw a van slowing down and moving directly towards us. From the van, I heard my mother call my name, "Ricky!" When I heard her voice my heart dropped to my stomach. At that moment, I knew that my mother was going to beat the living crap out of me. As I nervously and hesitantly walked towards the van, my mother snatched me into the van without even getting out herself. It was like she had a rubber arm. My mother put a beating on me like I was a human punching bag. She punched, slapped, kicked and hollered at me all at the same time. My mother was definitely no pushover.

The beating that I received that night did not stop me from gravitating towards the vices that destroyed a lot of my friends. The streets were calling my name and slowly reeling me into the abyss of destruction. I found myself skipping a class here and there. One class turned into two. Two classes turned into four, and eventually I just stopped going to school. I would leave the house pretending to go to school. Then I would meet up with some of the guys in the hood and just hang out all day. I did not plan to drop out of school. It just happened. Nobody grows up planning to go to prison, planning to be a murderer, or even becoming addicted to drugs. It's a combination of a person's environment, their choices and circumstances.

I truly appreciate the woman who brought me into this world. There were many mistakes, obstacles and uncomfortable circumstances; but I have never denied or even second-guessed my mother's love for me or my brothers. For as long as I can remember, my mother always kept a job, took care of us and would give her last to make sure that we wouldn't be without. There are times when I sensed that my mother lives with a lot of regret. But who doesn't? Shedding tears from the mistakes of the past seem to get the best of her, but I thank God that she's still standing in the midst of it all. My mother received the Lord Jesus Christ into her life; and yours truly was privileged to baptize her. What a wonderful experience for a son to baptize and now pastor his own mother! For years, she covered me, but now it is my time to cover her.

At age 48, I'm a husband, father, grandfather, father-in-law, businessman, college graduate, pastor and now an author. Thus, to answer my former question; "Yes, something good can come out of Detroit and plenty of good things have". Considering the odds that were stacked against me, there is no way that I should be here today. Jesus Christ, The Way, The Truth and The Life rescued me from darkness and chose me to be a part of His kingdom. The Holy Spirit dwells within me and empowers me to live out my faith on this earth.

CHAPTER 2

(Highlights Of My Life)

The 80's were probably one of the most tragic eras in black communities all across the country. The crack epidemic devastated communities, destroying the lives of individuals and sometimes wiped out entire families. Drugs, guns, murder and drug enterprises (such as, Young Boys Incorporated, Best Friends and other major drug king-pins) dominated the streets of Detroit and newspaper headlines. I, personally, believe that crack cocaine was systemically filtered into the black communities. I witnessed many of my friends, neighbors and family members succumb to the drug epidemic of the 1980's. Even today, black communities still haven't fully recovered.

In the 1980's, house and block parties were extremely popular. You could always find a good party somewhere in the neighborhood. Even at the age of thirteen I would go to some of the roughest and toughest neighborhoods just to get my pop-lockin', moonwalk and tick on. The world saw Michael Jackson perform the Moonwalk on Motown 25. But in the hood, the Moonwalk wasn't new to us.

One night while going to a party, my best friend and I were approached by a group of guys who were looking for a couple of other guys. Apparently, the night before the guys they were looking for jumped on someone they knew. And, yes, we fit the description. One of the guys brandished a gun and was being hyped up by his friends to bust a cap in us. I was so scared that I couldn't even move. My best friend, Frank, had the "gift of gab" and was known for his smooth talking, (especially when it came to the girls). Man, he was good! I knew he was nervous, but you would have never known it. The way he handled and defused the situation that night was truly amazing. It reminds me of Bill Cosby in the movie *Uptown Saturday Night*, when he talked his way out of several life-threatening situations. Almost ten years later, my best friend Frank, would be shot and killed. Who would have ever thought that yours truly would be the one offici- ating his funeral.

(FRANK & GEE)

Although I was associated with several guys in the hood, there were only two guys whom I considered myself to be very close to, and they were: Frank and Gee. Both of them were like night and day. Frank was cool, loved to dress, loved girls and was just a good guy. He wasn't a pushover and would fight if he had, but that wasn't his thing. His thing was partying, dancing, having a good time and enjoying life to the fullest. To this day, I don't remember Frank getting into one fight. All we wanted to do was dance, party, meet girls and enjoy life. Frank and I would go from hood-to- hood looking for parties and dance competitions. There was one characteristic Frank had that always impressed me, and that was his smooth-talking ability. The guy was good!

Gee, on the other hand, was the total opposite. He was known for his quick temper and loudness. Every time you turned around, Gee was in a fight or getting ready to fight. He seemed to have the mindset of always trying to prove that he wasn't a punk. Gee was also controlling and (to a degree) manipulative. He could get very angry if you did not agree with him or do what he wanted you to do. There were times when I found myself in the midst of an altercation because of him, and I had nothing to do with it. Whether we were at the recreation center, the playground or even at school, something was bound to jump off. The very first time I went to Eastland Shopping Mall, I was arrested for shoplifting. Gee and I went to Eastland to purchase some athletic wear. My mother gave me money to purchase my items, and I did. Meantime, Gee, was putting all types of items in his bag. He even asked me if I wanted something and (like a dummy) I said "Yes." As we were moving towards the door to exit the store, both of us were approached by security guards, and the rest is history. We were booked, our photos taken and a call was placed to our homes. In reality, I wasn't scared of the security guards; I was scared to face my mother. I knew that she was going to beat the living snot out of me, and she did. My mother made it very clear to me that she did not want me to hang around with Gee anymore. Although, I did not physically steal anything, I was just as guilty as Gee. I was guilty by association. A lot of my friends' lives were ruined because they were guilty by association.

(ALMOST CAUGHT UP)

As I stated, the 80's proved to be one of the most devastating eras in the black communities across this country. In the City of Detroit young black males were being recruited by one of the largest drug organizations, called YBI aka Young Boys Incorporated. YBI was known for wearing Adidas Top Tens, Adidas Shirts, Levi Jeans, gold jewelry and carrying wads of money. YBI built their multi-million dollar operation off the backs of young, impressionable teenage black males and murder.

There were times when I wanted to join YBI. Like most teenage boys that I grew up with in the hood, we were fascinated and mesmerized by the cars, money, clothes, shoes and the unity they displayed. What do you tell a young, black, hard-headed, teenage boy who comes from a single-parent home, with no direction or discipline, running the streets, and on top of everything else, broke? The odds were totally stacked against me. Though I was tempted, I never joined Young Boys Incorporated, and I thank God that I didn't. I tend to think that one of the reasons why Frank and I never joined YBI was because of the horrific stories that we heard in the streets about their Wrecking-Crew. If you messed up in any type of way (such as, stealing money, stealing product or selling drugs on their territory), the Wrecking-Crew would pay you and your family a visit. I did, however, start slinging drugs for a guy on the block named, Big Reg. Frank and I decided on slinging drugs for him. He was doing his own thing and we thought it would be much easier and safer. Little did we know Big Reg was just as dangerous and notorious as the others.

The very first time I was given a supply of drugs to sell, I ended up losing the product at a picnic. I was on the verge of losing my mind. I knew that I had to either find the product or come up with his money. I spent hours looking for the bag of weed that he supplied me. For days, I was ducking and dodging him. I knew that ducking and dodging him wouldn't last long. It would only be a matter of time before he came to my house to confront me about his product or money. One day, Big Reg spotted me and Frank walking down the street. He told us to come over there. He had a guy with him that Frank and I had never seen before. There were several things that I remembered about that guy. The first thing I noticed was the serious and deathly look that he had on his face.

He stared at us like he could see right through us, and he never blinked (at least I did not notice it). The second thing I noticed was the long, shining butcher's knife that he was twirling around while staring at both of us. Not one time did that guy smile, talk or blink. Big Reg introduced us to Mr. Death, so I thought, and proceeded to question us about his product and money. I do not remember what was said, but I do remember him telling both of us to come into his house. And, like idiots, we did. While Big Reg was talking about drugs, money, loyalty and what he would do to a person who crossed him, Mr. Death stared at us the whole time while twirling his knife. Big Reg made a statement that made my heart drop and my entire body weak. He said *"I don't mine killing a nigger and burying him in my basement."* When he made that statement, I could see Frank's hands shaking as he rolled a joint. I was completely numb because I just knew something was going to happen. But, once again, Frank and his masterful gift of gab got us out of that one.

I had to find a way to come up with Big Reg's money or else suffer the consequences. Sounds like "Smokey" in the movie *Friday*. Suffice to say I ended up stealing the money to pay off my debt with Big-Reg. It was then when I realized that selling drugs was not for me. There was too much pressure associated with it.

My entire family (for the most part) lived all over Detroit's eastside. By the time I was 13 years old, we probably moved about 20 or more times. No matter what neighborhood I

29

moved to, I was always able to socialize, mix and mingle with just about everybody. I made friends everywhere I moved. Moving so much gave me a huge advantage in so many different ways. Looking back now, I am so glad that we moved around a lot. I say this because I did not have time to get myself totally entrenched in the madness on the horizon. I had no idea that countless guys with whom I grew up, attended school and played sports, would end up becoming killers, being killed, maimed or incarcerated for years or even life.

Gee eventually became a big drug dealer with an attitude. He also became a killer. I remember going back to the hood just to drive around and reminisce. I drove down Gee's street. While driving, I saw him coming out of the house and getting into a car with his baby brother. I got out of the car, and we proceeded to have a conversation. I must admit that I was glad to see Gee. Our conversation did not last long, but it was long enough for me to convey to him about my new life, and I wasn't ashamed. I wasn't ashamed to tell Gee that I was in church, married and a minister. We shook hands and parted ways. A few months later, Gee's little brother was murdered. When I heard about it, I knew that he would go on a murderous rampage. If there was one person in Gee's life that he would kill or die for, it was his baby brother, his only sibling. I knew that given his quick temper, reputation and the love for his baby brother he would seek revenge on anyone who he thought had something to do with his brother's death. The word on the street was that Gee was on a murderous rampage and had killed several people whom he suspected of killing his little brother. Gee was arrested, jailed, but not charged in several murders. He was eventually bailed out of jail, but within a week he was brutally tortured and murdered. This was the same guy who I grew up with, hung out with, walked to and from school with, played basketball with, joked with and even helped with his paper route. I am 100% positive that if I had continued down the wrong path, I myself would have been a statistic.

Several years after Gee's death, something happened that literally threw me for a loop. My son, Julian, was having his kindergarten graduation ceremony. During the festivities that surrounded the ceremony, my son was playing with one of his classmates. As the teacher rounded up the students to call off their names to receive their kindergarten certificates, she called the name of the little boy who playing with my son. I immediately recognized the last name. He had the same last name as Gee's. Staring at him intensively, I could clearly see that this little boy who had been my son's classmate resembled Gee. When the ceremony was over, I asked the little boy's mother whether Gee was his father, and she said, "Yes." It was then that I further realized how good God had been to me. I realized that if it had not been for the grace and mercy of God, that same little boy could have been Julian. Although thankful, I couldn't help but feel compassion and anguish for the little boy who would grow up not knowing his father.

(SHOOT ME NIGGA)

We had a beef with some guys who lived in another neighborhood. Till this day, I really don't remember what the beef was all about. I think it was over a girl. Late one night, tempers were flaring and threats were being made (not to mention a whole lot of cussing). While trying to impress my friends and prove how tough I was, I did something that was completely stupid. One of the guys from the opposing side had a gun and was threatening to shoot us. Like an idiot, I walked towards the guy, stepped in front of him and dared him to shoot me. My adrenaline was on 10, and I was caught up in the moment and kept yelling *"Shoot me, Nigga!"* I even turned my back and repeated myself. I then pulled up my shirt, pointed at my chest and uttered the same words. How stupid can you get? Thank God that guy wasn't trying to prove himself. Every time I think about that moment, chills run down my spine.

CHAPTER 3

(My Father)

My father was a gangster back in the 1970's. While growing up, I heard many stories about his unsavory activities. My grandparents (especially my grandmother) made it very clear that they did not want me to be associated with my father because of his lifestyle. I had the opportunity to visit him while he was incarcerated. We sat down in one of the prison yards and started talking about me, how I was doing and staying out of trouble. My father repeatedly made it very clear to me never to be sentenced to prison. We agreed that when he got out of prison, we would connect to embark upon starting a real father and son relationship.

The opportunity presented itself with me getting to know him. In that process, I discovered that he had another son, my half-brother, who ended up becoming a big drug dealer. The last time I tried to see my half-brother was when he was in the hospital. There was an attempt made on his life, but he survived. I tried to visit him, but officers and guards would not allow it.

One day, while hanging out with my father, I witnessed something that totally blew me away. I don't know the circumstances surrounding that particular incident, but I witnessed my father beating another guy to a bloody pulp. The beating was so bad that it shook me to the core. I begged and pleaded with my father to stop, but he ignored me. The saddest thing about the entire situation was that nobody tried to stop it. Till this day, I honestly think my father did that to impress me. Little did he know I was not impressed, but confused and very disappointed. One minute he was talking and laughing with the guy, and the next minute he was beating the guy up.

(I SHOULD HAVE KNOCKED)

One day while out shopping with my grandmother, I asked if I could go and see my father, who only lived several blocks away. At first, my grandmother was hesitant, but after pleading with her, she gave me her permission. I was so happy that she did. You see, no matter what my father did and how my family felt about him, I still had a longing to get to know him. At that point, I had already gotten over the fact that he beat a guy in front of me. All I ever wanted was to build a relationship with my father. I ran over to his house, knocked on the door, spoke to my great grandmother and proceeded to go upstairs to my father's room. Instead of knocking, I opened the door and saw my father shooting drugs into his arm. I was so frightened by what I saw, that I ran out of the house without saying goodbye to my great grandmother and crying all the while. I heard my father call my name, but I kept on running. I gathered my emotions and never told my grandmother what happened. A few weeks later, I discovered that a hit was placed on my father's life. The perpetrator climbed through my father's window and tried to murder him. He woke up just in time and beat the man almost to death. A few months later my father was found dead in that very same room.

(HE LIVED AND DIED)

My father died when I was around fifteen years old. I attended his funeral and, quite naturally, cried. The first thing I noticed at my father's funeral was the length of his obituary. His obituary was only a paragraph and a half, maybe less. It was like he just existed and vanished without any relevant history. A father should leave a legacy to his family, so that they can have something to build upon and go further in life. Most of the things that I had ever heard about my father were negative. It was not until he died when I realized that I was left with nothing to build upon. The only thing I knew was that I wanted to be different. I realized that I would no longer have the opportunity of a relationship, a relationship that I so desperately longed for. The longing would go unfulfilled, and for this I felt cheated. I tend to believe that I cried mostly because what could have been wasn't, and the reality of anything materializing was forever gone. All of us must take into consideration that God provides us with many opportunities to "get it right", but it's up to us to do the work and "make it right." It was at my father's funeral that I made a conscious decision that I would move forward and seek God's plan for myself and my future family. The million-dollar question was, "How could I build a legacy for my future family, when I, myself, did not have a reference point?"

It was not until later in life that I discovered the main reason my grandparents did not want me to be associated with my father. After his death, it all came out. You see, when I was around seven years old, my father tried to physically assault my grandmother. I remember the entire situation surrounding this claim like it was yesterday. I remember waking up in the middle of the night to go to the bathroom. As I walked to the bathroom, I heard someone whisper my name from the back door window. The whispers got louder, but more direct and demanding. The man whispering at the door was my father. It was that night that he attempted to physically assault my grandmother. Thank God I didn't comply with my father's demands. That same night a huge-boulder came crashing through the side window. The next day my grandfather bought a gun.

As a child growing up, I always wondered about the scar on the side of my grandfather's eye. I also use to wonder why my grandfather could only move his arm a certain way. It looked stiff. It was not until my father died that I discovered he was the reason my grandfather's eye and arm looked the way that it did. My father physically assaulted my grandfather with a knife. Once I knew all of that, I totally and completely understood why my grandparents and family didn't care for him. I also understood why my two older brothers couldn't stand me mentioning my father's name around them. My oldest brother, who I looked up to, made it perfectly clear how he felt about my father. There were times when my oldest brother would tell me to shut up. He never wanted me to speak of my father around him.

My mother and grandmother kept those things from me, out of love, and for my protection. I wasn't angry, nor was I bitter against them. How could I be? After all, they were doing their job to keep me from the foolishness. Now that I recall, I never heard my grandparents, nor my mother speak negatively around me about my father. Mothers must be very careful not to say anything negative about their children's father. They may not be able to handle it and it could very well backfire on you. In one of my favorite movies, "*A Few Good Men*" the actor, Tom Cruise, was pressing Jack Nicholas to cough up the truth. Back and forth they went until Jack replies to Tom, "You can't handle the truth." Therefore, it behooves mothers to restrain from speaking negatively to their children about their father, especially boys, because they may not be able to handle it.

CHAPTER 4

(God Orchestrating My Life)

In 1983, the course of my life began to change. The first part of this transition took place when I decided to live with my grandmother. I never wanted to live with my grandmother simply because she was strict, a no-nonsense person, but loving and humorous at the same time. I had come to the realization that if I did not change my association and have some structure in my life, I would experience a point-of-no-return. Changing my associations would be the first step towards taking hold of my destiny and God's plan for me.

The decision that I made to live with my grandmother proved to be a turning point in my life. Deep down inside I was willing and ready to change the course of my life, and it all started with the simple decision of changing my surroundings. I knew that if nothing else my grandmother, Lois Mack-Dandridge, had my back and (most importantly) my best interests at heart. I knew that if I couldn't trust anybody else, I could trust her (no matter what). I knew that if I wanted my life to change, I had to willingly submit myself under her authority and do what I was told, including going to church. You see, my grandmother (although kind and sweet) didn't take any stuff from anybody. She was well-over 6 feet tall, could sing and swing, if you know what I mean. Madea did not have anything on my grandma. My grandma was the real deal. I saw her beat up my mother's boyfriend, and I remembered it like yesterday. There was an altercation between my mother and her boyfriend. I called my grandmother to notify her of the situation. My grandfather and grandmother came over to the house. My grandmother told my grandfather to wait in the car, while she took care of business. The next thing I heard and saw was furniture moving around. My grandmother was literally on top of my mother's boyfriend handling her business. She then ordered all of us to get in the car. As we drove off, I saw my mother's boyfriend with tears in his eyes. Grandma always made it clear that she did not want anybody messing with her grandchildren, especially if you're not taking care of them.

I can honestly say that going to church was something that our family did. My grandmother made sure that her grandchildren attended church, and quite frankly I've always enjoyed going to church, especially during Easter. As my brothers, cousins, and I grew older, attending church was few and far between. It must be noted that the church was always an important element in the black family. It was the black church that held families together, promoted education, started organizations, including historical black colleges. It was even the backbone of the Civil Rights Era.

(SPIRITUAL ENCOUNTER)

The decision to attend church was the second most important decision that I could have ever made. This decision positioned me to fill the emptiness in my life during that time. Not even my darling and loving grandmother could fill the void that was ever present in my life, even at the age of thirteen.

The first day that I attended church, I felt like I was on a mission. Out of all the times I attended church there was something completely different about attending that first time around. The church was New Maclin Temple COGIC (located at 2255 E. Forest) in Detroit, Michigan. It was at that small, but vibrant church that I would experience and encounter the grace, mercy and presence of God Almighty.

The late James M. Maclin, Sr., was the pastor at the time. I must say that he was truly a man of God, who walked in love, integrity and was known for his prayer life. My new surroundings consisted of singing, dancing, shouting and fervent preaching from Pastor Maclin and other ministers. I knew that church was the right place for me. There was no doubt in my mind that if I wanted my life to change and my future to be redirected, I needed to be in a safe place. Each time I attended church, the void in my life, and the longing were slowly dissipating. It was not until I willingly gave my life totally over to the Lord Jesus Christ that the void was completely filled. Sunday, December 11, 1983 was the day that the void in my life was filled and my future brighter. In every human being there is a space that can only be filled by God. My life and destiny have shifted; not because of my goodness, but because of God's grace and mercy.

There I was, in that small, but vibrant storefront church, broken and bruised. Little did I know, that small church would be the turning point of my entire life. From that day forward, I made up in my mind that I wanted to be different, and I wanted something different. No matter who you are, if you want things to change in your life, there are two things that you must do: change your associations, and your attitude. The scripture teaches us that "evil communication corrupts good manners." (I Corinthians 15:33).

During that time period, I was a high school dropout. One Sunday a deacon by the name of Willie Fair approached me about school. Deacon Fair commended me for being in church, getting involved and being a part of the church family. After doing so, he asked me one simple question, "Are you in school?" My response was, "No." Deacon Fair encouraged and challenged me to go back to school to obtain my high school diploma. The next day, I woke up early in the morning, got on the bus and personally enrolled myself back in school.

From that point on, my primary objective was to obtain my high school diploma. Nothing and no one was going to stand in my way. I was so determined to graduate, that I attended summer school, night school, classes on Saturday, and even volunteered at the church for extra credit. In 1986, I was blessed to walk across the stage and obtain my diploma from Edwin Denby High School. I will never forget the joy that my grandmother expressed during the commencement. She even gave me $200 to buy a suit, shoes, shirt and tie for the occasion. Finally, one of her grandsons had graduated from high school, and she lived to see it. Prior to her death, she encouraged me to continue to pursue my college degree. It was in honor of her memory, that I obtained a Bachelor's and Master's Degree. I also did it to set the tone for my children and the next generation of Sykes'.

It was during my last year of high school that I met my beautiful and intelligent wife, Christine Johnson. Her locker was across the hall from mine, but I never noticed her. It was not until a mutual friend introduced us. From that day, it was on and poppin'! Like "snap, crackle, pop!" From the moment we started talking, I knew that she was going to be my wife. Those big beautiful eyes, gorgeous smile, and her love for Jesus Christ is what did it for me. She knew what she wanted and I knew what I wanted.

There is another reason why I knew that Christine was going to be my bride. She came to school smelling like chicken, and I knew right then and there that she was the one for me. You see, my wife worked for KFC and (at times) she would wear a coat that smelled like chicken. I prayed and asked God to give me a sign that she was my wife, and she came to school the next day smelling like chicken. As a young minister at the time, I realized that this was an obvious sign seeing that the gospel bird (chicken) is king in African American churches. What greater sign did I need at the time? On November 14, 1987, we exchanged wedding vows in front of our family and friends. Besides accepting the Lord Jesus Christ as my personal savior, exchanging wedding vows with my lovely bride, Christine Johnson, was one of the happiest times in my life. She brought safety and stability to my life.

CHAPTER 5

(The Sykes Family Began)

"Lo, children are an heritage of the LORD:
and the fruit of the womb is his reward.
As arrows are in the hand of a mighty man;
so are children of the youth.
Happy is the man that hath his quiver full of them:
they shall not be ashamed,
but they shall speak with the enemies in the gate"
Psalm 127:3-5

In 1988, our first son, Ricky, Jr., was born. Not only did I witness the birth of my first born, but I was also the first to hold him as he smiled at me. It was at that moment when I realized that being in my child's life was primary. On that day, I also realized that my journey as a father had just begun. I think every man should experience the birth of a child. In 1990, our second son, Julian, was born. While at work I remembered getting a call to meet my wife at the hospital. By the time I got there, Julian was already on the way out. But I thank God I got a chance to witness his birth, as well. The fact that my wife delivered him really fast, told me a lot about him. I had a hunch that this little fellow was born with a strong will. In 1993, my son, Christian, was born. Christian was born three days before my grandmother's funeral. Although I was excited about my son's birth, I was also sad because my grandmother did not get a chance to see her new great-grandson. In 1995, my daughter, Kourtney, was born. That was one of the most joyous days of our lives. We finally had a girl! Having a daughter would prove to be challenging for me simply because I did not have the knowledge or skillset in terms of dealing with females. In 1998, my fourth son, Jalen, was born. Although I had the opportunity to witness his birth, I don't quite remember specific details that surrounded it. When Jalen was born, the dynamics of our family had shifted. It was during that time in our lives when a lot of things were going on. My wife was working full time while the other children were in school. The older boys were playing sports, and we were very much involved with various church activities. Jalen was very attached to his mother. In 2001, the Lord blessed us with another son, Caleb. We knew from the looks of my wife's stomach that Caleb would be a huge baby with a big head. Deep down inside I knew that this would be our last child. So, I purposely made sure that I was involved and enjoyed every aspect of my wife's pregnancy. My wife had to have a C-section because of the size of Caleb's head. I really didn't want to see her get cut on, so I allowed two of her closest friends to accompany her. At times, I do regret that I did not accompany my wife through the procedure. I am truly thankful to God that He blessed my wife and I with six healthy children. I am also thankful that he granted us the awesome responsibility of raising our own family. Raising a family is tedious and stressful, but the benefits are rewarding. There are sleepless and restless nights; but there are nights when peace will overshadow you, no matter how it looks.

I highly respect single mothers and all the grandmothers who have stepped in to fill the role of fathers. I know what my mother and grandmother had to endure in trying to raise five boys (eight if you count my cousins). Most of the issues that we are bombarded with today can be traced back to the fact that there are too many children whose fathers are not involved in their lives. There are too many young boys living without direction, discipline and support from fathers or father-figures.

I made a conscious decision that no matter what, I will be directly involved in the lives of our children. However, in order for me to accomplish this task, I knew that I would have to teach them the fundamentals of manhood (such as, respect, responsibility, honesty, honor, etc.). I knew that if I wanted them to grow up to be respectful, I must be their example. No one is perfect, but if we desire to get better positive results from our children, we must practice what we preach. When you do make a mistake, it's okay to admit it and apologize. Children (especially teenagers) will respect you to the highest level when you openly admit your mistakes and failures.

After 26 years of parenting and making mistakes along the way, I adopted seven teaching principles that I am confident will be a blessing to all families regardless of status, ethnicity, religious background or education. These seven principles can be summed up in the word, **T.H.R.E.A.D.S** (*Transparency, Honor, Responsibility, Example, Affirmation, Decision* and *Selflessness*). This book contains real-life situations and challenges that we, as a family and I, as a father, had to endure and work through. This book is not about perfect parenting, but about dealing with the many challenges of fatherhood (especially in the area of raising males). It is my prayer that you will find this information to be a blessing to you and your family.

CHAPTER 6

(Transparency)

But speaking the truth in love,
may grow up into him in all things,
which is the head, even Christ:
Ephesians 4:15

I strongly believe that in order for parents to have a good relationship with their children, they must be willing to be transparent with them. Transparency requires real conversation, truth, systematic dialogue and, yes, a willingness to admit mistakes. It has always been a lifelong commitment of my wife, and I to have real and honest conversations with our sons (and daughter). We realized that in order for us to better prepare them to live in a world that is flawed and perverse, truthful dialogue needs to take place on a consistent basis.

Sex is real. STD's are real. Drugs are real. Racism, discrimination, police brutality, crime, perversity and unemployment are all real issues; and they require us, as parents, to have real and honest conversations with our sons and daughters. There was a time when parents could (for the most part) shield their children from certain things. Not any longer! Those days are forever gone! The access to 24-hour cable television, the internet, social media and other mass media outlets have made it virtually impossible for parents to shield their children from the gross immorality that constantly bombards us. With a simple click of a button your child could be exposed to images that could possibly impact their entire life. Therefore, it's imperative that we, as parents, keep it real with our children concerning various subject matters that continue to plague our society. As a father, I kept it real with my children even though, at times, the conversations were very uncomfortable. With regards to racism and discrimination, I have always kept it real with them, even to this very day. From the time they started driving, I kept it real as it relates to being stopped by the police. My conversation with them was plain and simple "You will get stopped by the police." I try my hardest not to get sucked into the various racial issues, tension, discrimination and the like. But for me to ignore it would be irresponsible on my part. The concept of DWB (Driving While Black), can be debated until the cows come home. The fact of the matter is, we must teach our children how to avoid as well as handled confrontation. For example, I made it very clear to my sons, that when stopped by a police officer, be respectful, keep your head and be smart. The main objective was to arrive safely to your destination, not to prove your manhood. Too many young brothers have lost their lives either trying to prove their manhood, being ill-informed and just downright foolish. Transparency is not about making a person feel good. Transparency is about educating and empowering individuals to understand and become more responsible. I began the sex talk with my sons while they were in middle school. Little did I know they were already exposed to and had done things that we tried to keep them away from. The things that they shared with me, literally blew me away. I discovered that the females were more aggressive than the boys. Back in the day, I was lucky to get a kiss in middle school, let alone have sex with a girl. Times have definitely changed. The sex conversation can be uncomfortable, but it is one conversation that you and I must have. The reason for this is due to the fact that every time sex is mentioned, it is primarily from a negative connotation rather than from a positive one. Sex was created by God and is meant to be enjoyed, pleasurable and for procreation within the confines of marriage. Therefore, when discussing serious matters with our children, we must always convey the pros and the cons. Balanced conversation equates to healthy conversation. As a Christian minister, my sons know what my message is concerning sex; and that is "No sex before marriage." It's easier said than done, especially when you're an athlete, around lots of girls vying for your attention and not to mention a preacher's son. I know that it can be done because the Bible says you can do it. But when you are constantly bombarded with images from every end of the spectrum, it makes it that much more difficult for any young man to fight temptation. I told my sons that the best feeling in the world is sex. There is absolutely nothing that you can compare it to or with. No matter how educated you are "sex" cannot be explained. And once you engage in it there is no telling where it will lead to. There is a reason why the Bible tells us to flee fornication, not commit adultery and reject all other sexual practices. History tells us that families, homes, churches, businesses, reputations and lives have been destroyed because of adultery, fornication, pornography, etc.

One of the most powerful informal sessions that I had with my three older boys took place while we were working in the yard. We were just having a casual conversation and suddenly the subject matter switched to sex. For me that wasn't a preaching or teaching moment, but more of a listening one. Listening is a big part of parenting. I listened as my two older sons talked about their many sexual experiences and encounters with women. As they went on and on, both of them made a statement that almost floored me. They alluded to the fact that they wished they had never engaged in having sex until marriage. I then asked them why they had felt that way. In a nutshell both of them said that they felt dirty, empty and that they lost something that they couldn't recover. Man, those were some powerful words, especially coming from young men. Meanwhile, my two older sons encouraged their younger brother not to engage in any sexual activities till marriage. The fact that they were transparent in sharing their feelings, allowed me to gain a better insight into their characters. Most importantly my message on "Wait until marriage" had resonated with them.

I was extremely disappointed when I found out that my oldest son had impregnated a young lady. I wasn't surprised, but I was very much disappointed. I learned that no matter how much a person tries to guard their family, children and even their image unexpected circumstances will occur. The anger, disappointment and frustration that follow these unexpected circumstances are real and must not be ignored. I told my son how angry and disappointed I was with his actions and especially for violating another man's daughter. I know that it takes two to tangle, but that still does not negate the fact that breaking the cycle of unwed mothers and children born out of wedlock requires discipline and responsibility. Transparency afforded me the opportunity to express to him how I felt, and at the same time, let him know that as a family we will get through this together. I took it a step further by meeting with the father and mother of the young lady who my son impregnated. I deeply apologized for my son's actions and assured them both that my son would take full responsibility and do the right thing. I felt that it was my duty to meet her father face-to-face in order to express my position and establish a relationship for the benefit of the child. I felt that the future of our grandchild will be determined by our ability to get along, regardless of the unexpected circumstances.

Whatever the subject matter, transparency allows us to be real, not only with our children, but with ourselves. Transparency will enable us to build a healthy relationship with our sons and daughters by "speaking the truth in love." I have discovered that when I am transparent with my children, they are more open to being receptive to my advice and guidance. My biblical insight, personal experience, as well as, my mistakes allow me to understand their world, be relatable, relevant and patient.

One of the beauties of the Bible is that it is filled with so many transparencies. It tells us about the faith, failures and flaws of many great men and women. The Bible doesn't try to hide the fact that Noah had a drinking problem, Moses had anger issues, and Samson struggled with lust and David's affair with Bathsheba. In fact, David's scandal affected his empire. Each one of these individuals were rebuked and even suffered the consequences for their actions. But it was their faith in God, repentance and transparency that caused them to rise above their failures and flaws. Psalms 51 is about David's transparency with himself and the living God of Israel.

To be transparent regarding this matter means that we are:

- Committed to speaking the truth in love
- Forthright about our flaws and mistakes
- Engaging in systematic dialogue about real issues
- Understanding the world in which your child lives
- Spending more time on the relationship than on rules

CHAPTER 7

(Honor)

"The fear of the LORD is the beginning of knowledge:
but fools despise wisdom and instruction"
Proverbs 1:7

I recommend that every young person read and meditate on the Book of Proverbs, for it contains biblical instructions that apply to every facet of our lives. The book was written by King Solomon, one of the greatest (not to mention) the wisest king who ever lived. The Book of Proverbs talks about diligence, laziness, debt, wisdom, foolishness, honor and controlling anger and tongue. The Biblical passage listed above literally set the tone of the entire book and one's life. The word "fear" means to hold in high esteem, respect, reverence, honor or to take seriously. Having a true fear of God will greatly impact every aspect of a person's life.

As a Christian, I believe that everything starts with fearing God. I am of the mindset that everything starts with acknowledging the fact that there is a Creator who governs and rules all creation. This same Creator is not just governing the universe, but He is also keeping a record of every thought and action of all mankind. Fearing the Lord allows me to understand that one day I will have to give an account to a holy and just God, who is no respecter of persons. Every person who has ever lived will someday give an account to the Creator of the universe.

This same Creator gave us the Ten Commandments, one of which instructs children to honor their parents. In fact, the Lord was so serious about the matter, that he attached a promise to the commandment and that promise consisted of living out your days upon the earth. Exodus 20:12 *"Honor thy father and thy mother: that thy days may be long upon the land which the LORD thy God giveth thee.* In other words, the Lord has given every man an appointed time to die. Failure to honor ones parents will result in him or her not living out their appointed time on earth.

Honoring one's parents is important because it literally sets the tone both in the home and society, as a whole. If a child does not honor his or her parents, how in the world will they honor anyone else? Children must be taught and constantly reminded of who's in charge. Furthermore, they must be made to understand it's definitely not them. There must be a clear distinction between who's the father, the mother and the child. There can be no confusion, none whatsoever.

One of the main reasons there is so much chaos and confusion in homes, schools, neighborhoods and in our world today is because of the lack of honor (which, in essence, means respect). The lack of respect for parents, the elderly, teachers, police officers and judges is overwhelmingly oppressing. Newspaper articles are filled with stories of children killing their parents. There is no respect for human life. Social media has made it possible for our children to witness murder, violence and other ungodly activities.

I made it very clear to my children that disrespect will not be tolerated. Disrespecting their mother, teachers and grown folks period was grounds for immediate discipline. Their mother suffered and struggled birthing them into this world, and there was no way I was going to allow them to disrespect her. Honor is so dear to my heart, that I made it a personal mission of mine never to deal with grown-folks' matters in front of them. The objective was to set a precedent of respect and establish that children should know their place and stay of out of grown-folks' business. Honor is not about who is right or wrong. We can agree to disagree. We must always remember that one's approach and attitude towards any given situation is what matters most. I have always taught my sons that it does not matter what the issue is. Your approach and attitude will (for the most part) determine the outcome.

As we pursue this mindset of honor there are five key factors that we must all consider, and they are: (1) What is the premise? (2) Knowing your place, (3) Recognizing the person (4) Understanding the position (or situation); (5) Ultimately, who has the power? Following these steps will prevent and curb some of the madness that we see today (both in our homes and society).

One day, while driving, I was pulled over by the police. My wife and son Julian, were with me at the time. In all honesty, I had no idea why I was being pulled over, nor did they. When the officer approached the window, I politely asked him why I was being pulled over. Till this very day, I still don't know why I was stopped. The officer then asked me if I was the owner of the vehicle, did I have a warrant out for my arrest and a couple of other things. I felt myself getting very heated and even asked the officer why he asked me those types of questions. I respectfully replied to all of his requests, and he gave me a ticket for impeding traffic. Meanwhile, my son, Julian, was fuming and wasn't shy about letting the police officer know how he felt about my being pulled over. I told my son to calm down and let me handle the situation, but he kept on complaining. Finally, my fatherly instinct kicked into overdrive and demanded that he "shut up" before I "jacked him up." He complied. At that moment, the ticket didn't even matter to me anymore. What mattered to me most was the fact that my son did not understand his place. The position that he could have put himself in along with his parents, would have been costly. In reality he did not understand the power (or authority) of the person with the badge and gun. It didn't matter what the premise was. The fact is, the entire situation could have gotten out of hand. I knew right then and there that I had to teach my son to always respect authority, keep his head and know his place.

CHAPTER 8

(Responsibility)

When I was a child, I talked like a child, I thought like a
child, I reasoned like a child. When I became a man,
I put the ways of childhood behind me.
I Corinthians 13:11

Teaching children what it means to be responsible is a very important component of shaping their character. Teaching children to be responsible requires consistency and (most definitely) patience. Simple things (such as cleaning and picking up after themselves, helping out around the house, doing their homework and being honest) will teach children the fundamentals of responsibility. God expects us, as parents, to teach and nurture our children, especially when it comes to doing what is right.

In the process of teaching and nurturing our children, we must convey to them that life doesn't revolve around them.

There are responsibilities that go along with growing up in an ever-changing world. Children must understand that being irresponsible will equate to unnecessary trouble, suffering and heartache. There are certain areas in which I feel parents must convey the message of responsibility:

- Putting God first
- Following through with chores
- Prioritizing activities
- Understanding and saving money
- Honoring parents and authoritative figures
- Reading and learning how to listen
- Cultivating good friendships and relationships
- Honoring their word

Out of all my children, Julian (the second oldest), was probably the most difficult one to raise. He was hyper, driven, strong-willed, had a quick-temper, but very intelligent, musically and athletically inclined. In the sixth grade, he led a protest at a school that did not recognize or celebrate MLK Day. In this very same school, he was called a nigger by a white student. He broke the student's nose, was kicked out of school and was on the verge of being prosecuted. Getting into fights at school was constant. We would get call after call about Julian's fighting antics. All of this took place between elementary and middle school. My wife and I were both tired of the phone calls. I worked during the day and I couldn't keep taking long-lunch breaks in order to handle issues that Julian had.

I came to terms with the fact that if I did not take full responsibility in dealing with my son's quick temper and lack of self-control, the consequences could and would be devastating. I realized that if I did not deal with the heart of the matter, my heart and my wife's heart would be broken. We can either take responsibility to deal with or ignore issues now, but please be assured that these same issues will come back to haunt or hurt us later. I took time out to know my son, address those negative traits and habits, but at the same time cultivate his strengths. Whenever he did something out of line, I made him take full responsibility for his actions. I put both of my sons on the football team for the express purpose of channeling their aggression, as well as, learn the value of hard work and teamwork. Taking responsibility and being consistent proved to be the turning point for Julian. He became an outstanding wide-receiver. In addition, he was recruited to play football and basketball.

Two months before leaving for school, Julian did something that could have ruined his chances to play basketball. Not only could he have ruined his chances to play basketball, but he could have killed himself or someone else. I allowed Julian to use the car to hang out with some of his friends before he went off to college. I gave him a curfew with specific instructions and the whole nine yards. Not only did he disobey my instructions, but he was pulled over by the police because they witnessed him swerving. He was driving under the influence, under-age at the time and in the suburbs. Seven officers or more were on the scene, and all of them were Caucasian. Thanks be to God that one of the officers called me to inform me of the situation.

The Lord demonstrated His grace towards us by allowing my wife and I to pick up Julian and retrieve the vehicle without any legal ramifications. I tend to think that the officer gave him a break because they knew he was a former athlete at the local high school. Whatever the reason, this single, irresponsible act could have cost me thousands of dollars, but most importantly, it could have resulted in the loss of his life or someone else's. Children must understand that being irresponsible at any level can cost them a great deal. It could cost them their life, health, freedom, reputation, opportunities and even jeopardize good relationships.

No, Julian, didn't always get it right. And, yes, mistakes were made along the way. But I am proud to say that my son has turned out to be a mature, outstanding and strong man, husband, praise/worship leader and minister. He's blessed with a beautiful wife, and I know that they are going to do well in life. God is more than good. He's amazing!

CHAPTER 9

(Example)

Don't let anyone look down on you because you are young,
but set an example for the believers in speech, in conduct,
in love, in faith and in purity.
1 Timothy 4:12

Parents can no longer get away with the "Do as I say, not as I do" message. That time is over. We, as parents, must understand that children are watching almost everything that we say, do and don't do. I think that there are some parents who literally owe their sons and daughters apologies for saying one thing and doing another. We must lead by example. But as we lead by example, we must be willing to admit our flaws and mistakes. No one is perfect. Remember, transparency is the key, not perfection. Being an example to our sons and daughters requires living and demonstrating a consistent pattern of doing what is right. I have discovered that my sons respected me more when I admitted my flaws and mistakes.

If we desire for our sons and daughters to be loyal, then we, also, must live a life of loyalty. If we desire for our sons and daughters to be honest, then we, too, must practice honesty. If we want our sons and daughters to be respectful, then we, too, must be respectful. If we want our sons and daughters to value friendships, education and live a life of discipline, then we, too, must model these things. To be an example means that we, as parents, must demonstrate or model the core values that we desire to see in our children. Your children may not follow your paths in terms of occupation or aspirations. But what they can follow are those core values such as, integrity, respect, work ethics, dignity and all of those core values that ultimately define one's life. Fathers must teach their sons, what it means to be a real man. Fathers must be the example of responsibility, respect and doing what is right, even in pressure situations. By the same token, fathers and mothers must teach their daughters how to value themselves in every way.

Not too long ago, my sons and I went out to breakfast. My youngest son, Caleb, was riding with me. While backing out of the parking lot, I accidentally, but slightly bumped the car next to me. I got out of the car to check both cars for possible dents, marks or scratches. After I examined both cars, I came to the conclusion that the matter was minute' and was debating as to whether I should drive off. The more I thought about it, the more I realized that driving off would be unwise because it could possibly send my son the wrong message. My conscience would not allow me to drive off until I notified the driver of the other vehicle. I could have ignored the matter altogether and driven off, but I could not take the chance of sending my son the wrong message. There will come a point in each of our lives when we will have one shot to impact the lives of our children by a single action or decision. On that day, I chose to do the right thing. The entire situation wasn't really about a scuffed bumper, but rather about demonstrating to my son the importance of being honest and living with integrity. That was truly a teaching moment, and I am so glad that I chose to "do" rather than "say."

Caleb is the baby boy. I use to call him my little fat man, but now he's taller than me. He's a quiet giant. I see a lot of great things in him. Come to think of it, besides having his head in video games, Caleb really doesn't give his mother or me any trouble. Sometimes the older boys accuse me of being too soft on Caleb. And, honestly I am. Caleb is not my favorite. He just happens to be the baby, and along with that comes perks. Haven't they read the story of Joseph?

My son, Jalen, had an opportunity to play basketball and make a tremendous impact on a high school. The school had lost a couple of star players, and they needed someone to fill the void. They were looking for a player over six feet tall, athletic and who could be a threat (both offensively and defensively). Jalen fit the bill and then some. The entire family was excited about the possibilities of Jalen being under a good coach in a top Detroit school. There was one problem, we did not live in the school district. There were many options presented to enable us to beat and circumvent the system. However, those options did not line up with my Biblical beliefs, values and conscience. I would be lying to say I did not struggle with the decision. After all, who wouldn't want their son to play for a great coach in a program that has a history of pushing and producing great student athletes? Rationalization was at the center of my thought process. I came to the conclusion that setting a good example and precedent for my son was more important to me than anything. I declined the options offered. In my effort to obtain Jalen's perspective on the matter, I asked him how he felt about the situation and options presented. To my surprise, he agreed that doing the right thing was most important. What really blew me away was when he said that he didn't want anything to come back on him and us as a family. I must say that I was extremely proud of him that day. Jalen's statement, alone, told me a lot about his character. One of the great joys of being a father is seeing our children exhibit, good qualities, such as honesty, integrity, determination and respect, etc.

A few years ago, I experienced one of the most difficult and painful periods of my life. The pain and hurt was so severe that I couldn't sleep, eat or enjoy intimate moments with my wife. My character, reputation and livelihood were being severely threatened by someone who was extremely dear to me. And to make matters worse, I couldn't defend myself. My two older sons were privy to the whole situation. They got the news before I did. This was probably the first time that my sons witnessed their father becoming overwhelmingly heartbroken and depressed. I found myself slipping into a state of deep depression, and I could not help it. My sons were extremely angry and bitter about the entire situation. Not only were they shocked, but in a state of disbelief, as well. They could not understand why a person who I honored and loved so deeply, would do or allow such a thing.

It was during this time that I developed a life of prayer. I would go in the basement, fall prostrate on the cold floor and cry out to God. There were times when I felt like God wasn't hearing my plea for understanding, help, and vindication. But I kept praying and asking for deliverance or the wisdom to navigate through this thing that was threatening my character, reputation and livelihood.

The Lord heard my cry! The first thing that the Lord impressed upon me was to forgive. Even though I could not understand why I was going through this situation, the Lord revealed to me that forgiveness was the key to being healed. I was hurt, my character was being attacked, my reputation ruined and livelihood threatened. I realized that I had no right to harbor anger, unforgiveness and bitterness in my heart. What would Jesus do? With the help of the Lord, I pulled myself together, humbled myself and handled the matter like a godly man, and in the process of time, taught my sons about the essence of forgiveness. If you want God to operate in your life, you must learn to forgive and move on. Let go and let God. Areas of setting good examples are as follows:

- Honesty
- Respectful
- Self-control
- Patience
- Keeping your word
- Forgiveness

CHAPTER 10

(Affirmation)

*"And lo a voice from heaven saying, this is my beloved Son,
in whom I am well pleased."*
Matthew 3:17

One of the most difficult periods in my life was between the age of 17 and 30. Although I was married and employed, had children, bought my first home and I was a faithful church member, there was something deeply missing in my life. I wasn't sad, nor was I confused about who I was as a person. I knew I loved my family and the life that I was living as a Christian. I was around great people (both men and women) and can name countless men and women who greatly impacted my life on so many different levels. However, that did not negate the fact that there was something missing in my life which I could not explain. Finally, it came to me as clear as day. I can't tell when, or where. All I can tell you is that I received divine insight as to the reason this inexplicable void existed. You see, throughout my entire life I never had the esteemed honor of being affirmed by a father or father-figure. The emptiness that I felt inside had nothing to do with my love for family or even my church. It had everything to do with the fact that I didn't have a father in my life to affirm who I was, as a man. I had great mentors and examples in my life. There is nothing like having a father or father-figure who could speak into your life, systematically walk you through the steps of manhood and utter words of approval, as well as correction.

Sons and daughters must experience affirmation from their parents. Affirmation involves approving, validating, declaring, confirming, truthfulness and correcting. A key element in developing a healthy relationship with your children is affirmation. One of the things that I had to learn (as a father) was not to criticize or critique my children every chance I got. I realized that more time should be spent on affirming their strengths, yet at the same time helping them improve upon their weaknesses. Parenting is a lifelong journey. Therefore, we (as parents), must allow room for growth, freedom and mistakes.

As a Bible-believing Christian and pastor, I must always draw from biblical examples to convey points. I believe that Jesus, the Christ, is the Son of God and God-Incarnate (according to John 1:1-14). Even He experienced affirmation from God, the Father.

"*And lo a voice from heaven saying, this is my beloved Son, in whom I am well pleased.*" (Matthew 3:17)

"*While He yet spake, behold, a bright cloud overshadowed them; and behold a voice out of the cloud, which said, this is my beloved Son, in whom I am well pleased; hear ye Him.*" (Matthew 17:5)

If Jesus, the Son of God, God-Incarnate experienced affirmation from His Father, what about our sons and daughters? Jesus was perfect and sinless in every sense of the word, but affirmation has nothing to do with perfection. It has everything to do with strengthening, encouraging, empowering and correcting. Affirmation is what I was missing in my own personal life. I never had that father or father-figure in my life to say to me, "This is my beloved son, in whom I am well pleased. In other words, I am proud of you. You're doing a good job. Keep up the good work. Stay strong. tighten this area up", etc. Sons and daughters need to hear affirmation from their parents.

I made it my personal agenda to affirm my sons and my daughter. Every now and then I send out a text message, or personally inform each one of them that I am pleased, (especially when they have done something admirable or progressed in a certain area). No, they don't always get it right. And, yes, each one of them has made minor and major blunders. But again, affirmation involves approving, as well as, correcting. I would be an unwise father if I praised my sons and daughter for their mistakes, poor decisions or even their lifestyle that isn't biblically correct. I can praise them for their strengths, accomplishments, efforts and abilities.

My oldest son, Rick, Jr., knows what my expectations are of him. I have always taught him that being the firstborn child carries a tremendous responsibility. The relationship that I established with Rick, Jr., would set the tone for the rest of the children. As a result of my expectations, I found myself critiquing and criticizing him every chance I got. I praised him, at times; but suffice to say, I spent more time focusing on his weaknesses and mistakes, rather than his strengths. Critiquing and criticizing became the norm. It got to the point when every time I wanted to speak to him, he would reply, "*Is something wrong?*" I finally realized that the problem wasn't my son. It was me. If I wanted to change the dynamics of my relationship with my son and his "Is something wrong?" mentality, I must change my approach. Rather than spend time and energy focusing on his weaknesses and mistakes, I began to focus more on his strengths, accomplishments and efforts. I started affirming him, rather than always correcting him. Every now and then I would say to him "*I am proud of you!*" These 5 simple words literally changed the dynamics of our relationship.

When was the last time your son or daughter heard you say, "*I am proud of you.*" They may not be all that you want them to be, but at least try to identify one area in their life that they do well in. What about that son or daughter who has completely disregarded everything that you have taught them? They are living a life that is totally opposite of the values that you instilled in them. What about the father and mother who feel that they have failed their children by not being a good example or not being there at all? I believe that affirmation also involves forgiveness and healing. You must forgive yourself, ask for forgiveness, forgive your children and (prayerfully) seek other ways to make things right.

There was a time when I thought and believed that all of the positive instructions that I gave to my oldest son were futile. He grew up in the church, attended Sunday school, had good parents and was surrounded by a slew of men and women, who were godly examples men and women. But (for some reason) he was going in a totally opposite direction, especially after graduating from high school and going off to college. Plenty of times I was on the verge of putting him out of my house because of his rebelliousness and the foolishness along with it. Don't get me wrong, Rick never physically rose up against me, nor did he talk back to me. He was working and bought himself a car. But the direction in which he was going wasn't what I had planned. He was coming home after curfew, not answering his phone, hanging out at clubs, drinking; and every 60-90 days, there was a different girl. The life he was living and the example that he was setting in front of his brothers and sister were tearing me apart.

My son did me a favor when he decided to move out on his own freewill. But deep down inside, I knew he would return home. He eased his way back in by coming over to the house everyday to visit. This was his way of saying, "I'm ready to come back home." One reason he came back home is because there was no way in the world that he was going to find anybody who could cook like his mother. In March, 2010, the Lord spoke to me while I was in prayer. I heard an audible voice saying, "*I will chastise your son, but he will not die.*" Startled at what I had just heard, I looked around to see who had come into the room, but there was no one. I told my wife what I had heard. Later that day, Rick came home, and I proceeded to tell him what I heard. I warned him that because of his rebelliousness, disobedience and destructive habits, the Lord was going to chastise him, but he would not die. From that day forward, I **gave** him into the hands of the Lord.

August 10, 2010 was a day that I shall never ever forget. It was around 7 a.m., when my son, Julian, knocked on our bedroom door. He asked me whether he could use the car to go somewhere. From the look on his face I could tell that something was wrong. I asked him what's going on and why he needed the car at 7 a.m. in the morning. After pressing him, he finally told me that he got a call that Rick was in an accident and in the hospital. I was confused as to why no one called me or his mother about the situation. Julian told me that someone had been trying to call me all that morning, but it was going straight to voice mail. I looked at my phone and (for sure), it was dead. The night before I was preparing a sermon and forgot to charge my phone. Rushing to get to the hospital and charging my phone all at the same time, I finally got enough juice to turn the phone on. When I turned on my phone, lo and behold my voicemail was full of messages about my son being in the hospital. The accident happened at around 4 a.m., but we didn't get the news until around 7 a.m.

Rushing to the hospital, I saw heavy traffic, a fire truck, tow truck and police cars. Looking from a distance, I assumed that there was another accident. But as we drove by, I noticed that the vehicle on the other side of the road was mine. When I looked at the condition of the car, my heart almost stopped. There was no way in the world that my son could have lived. My rushing to the hospital quickly turned into a slow and somber cruise. I was completely numb and braced myself for the reality that I had lost my firstborn son. All I could think about was the first day that I held him in my arms as he smiled at me. Broken-hearted and at a loss for words, I begged God to please spare my son's life. I told the Lord that I could handle being talked about, lied on or even losing my home; but there is no way in the world I could handle losing my son. We arrived at the hospital only to discover that my son and his friend were severely injured. I had no idea that there was someone riding with him until that moment. My wife and I prayed for the both of them and began to thank the Lord for sparing both of their lives.

Yes, my son, Rick, and his friend were almost tragically killed in a traffic accident as they were t-boned by a semi-truck. The circumstances surrounding the accident included alcohol. My son was charged with an OWI (Operating While under the Influence), a 5- year felony. There were many legal debates as to my son's toxicology report, who was at fault and the police's failure to conduct a thorough investigation. Although my son's story was consistent as to what he had to drink that day, the report read that he "could have" been under the influence. Several times I questioned him about the accident and circumstances surrounding it. To this day I am still grateful that he and the young lady's lives were spared. God is more than good, He is amazing!

I must admit that although I was grateful, I was also angry and hurt that my son got himself into a real sticky situation. I was also angry with the fact that what I had been trying to build from scratch was being jeopardized by his careless-ness. Internally, I found myself more concerned about my legacy and image, than my son's situation. I was concerned with thoughts of what people will think or say, and so forth. I did some soul searching and reached the conclusion that this situation wasn't about me, but it was about being there for my son. I came to the realization that I needed to be by my son's side as he traveled this tedious journey. I remember looking into his eyes and ensuring him that no matter who, what, when and how, I would be right by his side every step of the way.

As parents, we must be there for our sons and daughters, even when they find themselves in the most difficult and delicate situations. This is also affirmation. It was during this defining moment that my son and I, not only developed a deeper father and son relationship, but a friendship. The strength, endurance and patience that my son displayed during the entire proceedings caused me to admire him. Everything I needed to know about my son was accomplished during this time of his life. He showed me that he was strong and that when faced with opposition, he will not run. The Lord worked it out, and now his life is back on track.

CHAPTER 11

(Decisions)

"Where there is no counsel, the people fall;
But in the multitude of counselors there is safety."
Proverbs 11:14

D ecisions are a part of everyday life. However, the results of the decisions that we make can prove to be successful or devastating. In fact, some of us are still dealing with some of the side effects of the decisions we've made in the past. This is why it's critically important that we constantly teach our sons and daughters about the importance of making good decisions. I have always taught my sons that for every decision made, there is a repercussion. Making the wrong decision can take a lifetime to recover from, if you recover at all. Therefore, it behooves parents to establish and cultivate a healthy relationship with their children. So, when the time comes for those crossroad decisions, our children will have the confidence in our ability to assist them with making the right decision. Decisions made in a vacuum can be costly.

Most of us have complicated our lives by making rash and emotional decisions. We find ourselves in uncomfortable and compromising situations due to poor decisions. If we desire our children to have confidence in our ability to help them, then we must develop a pattern of making good decisions ourselves. Decisions are so critical, that the Bible provides us with a blueprint in order to prevent us from making the wrong decision.

"Trust in the Lord with all your heart, and do not lean on your own understanding. In all your ways acknowledge Him, and He will make straight your path". (Proverbs 3:5-6)

"Where there is no counsel, the people fall; But in the multitude of counselors there is safety". (Proverbs 11:14)

"If any of you lack wisdom, let him ask God, who gives generously to all without reproach and it will be given him". (James 1:5)

There are several elements that we can glean from these three biblical passages: trusting and acknowledging God in everything that we do (before we do it), seeking godly counsel and asking God for wisdom. Over time, I have aimed to put into practice these biblical principles into my own personal life. Not only have I applied these principles in my own personal life, but I constantly convey them to my sons. You limit your mistakes by seeking and waiting on God. David, Israel's second king made, it his lifestyle to seek God about everything. Solomon, David's son, asked God for wisdom and understanding.

Decisions are critical, and so it's imperative that every one of us seeks God about everything. We must seek God about education, finances, marriage, opportunities and how to assist our sons and daughters as they navigate through life. I believe that decisions fall into three categories (1) decisions under pressure; (2) decisions for perception and (3) decisions for pleasure. I am only going to deal with "decision under pressure" simply because most of us are guilty of making decisions under pressure.

I have always taught my sons (and daughter) to never make decisions under pressure. Emotional decisions and decisions under pressure will come back to hurt or haunt you, for the most part. I am a firm believer that there is a solution to almost every situation and problem. The issue isn't the problem or situation, but our unwillingness to seek God, wait patiently and allow the problem to work through us or us working through the problem. Therefore, we make matters worse by making one bad decision after another.

The family was struggling immensely. Everyone felt the pressure of trying to make things happen in our household.

My oldest son was almost killed in a car accident, college expenses, house payments and other financial obligations. In his effort of trying to help the family meet various financial obligations, my son, Christian, got himself entangled in a scam. The scam cost him hundreds of dollars, and his identity was being compromised. Embarrassed and frustrated, he told me about the situation. I applauded his efforts in trying to help out the family, but I was disappointed with the fact that he failed to utilize the established procedure that is a core element in our home.

You see, Christian broke a cardinal rule by failing to seek counsel from me, his mother or even his two older brothers. In the Sykes' household, asking questions and seeking advice is an established rule. He made a decision under pressure. It cost him hundreds of dollars. And he almost lost identity. We had a family meeting to discuss the matter and reaffirmed the procedure for making decisions. Decisions made under pressure can cost a person a great deal. Therefore, it behooves all of us to seek God about everything, and then wait for the answer. One of Christian's greatest characteristics is his willingness to serve and help people. I love that about my son. But because of his generosity, there are times in which I feel like people would always try to take advantage of him; mistaking his meekness for weakness. Knowing this about him, I have to teach him balance, ask important questions and make sure that he doesn't make pressured decisions. If the President of the United States can seek counsel from those within his inner-circle, then we too, should adopt this same principle.

When Christian was a baby, he would always gravitate towards the stove. He would speed around the house in his walker, crash into people, make his way to the kitchen and gravitate towards the stove. Every single time my, wife would catch him, spank his hand and send him on his way. It didn't matter how many times she spanked him, he would always make his way towards the stove. There were times when I would catch him and spank him on the hand. After several times of going through the same routine, I decided to teach him a lesson. One day, while cooking food in the oven, my wife had to leave to run some errands. She gave me instructions as to when to turn the oven off and to make sure I watched Christian. This was my big break! It was the moment that I had been waiting for. Finally, the issue with his trying to touch the oven door would be rectified once and for all.

Like always, Christian made his way to the kitchen, and I followed him. He gradually moved towards the stove, looked at me as if to say *"You're not going to stop me"*. Moving towards the stove and looking at me all at the same time, he further made me believe in the doctrine of "original sin." I proceeded to let him touch the stove, and the expression on his face told me that he finally got the message. From that point on, we never had a problem with Christian gravitating towards the stove. He realized that, "it was too hot to handle".

As hard as we try to prevent and protect our children from hurt and harm, there will come a time when they will have to learn the hard way. Sometimes, by letting your children touch the stove; they will (hopefully) get the point and back away. Therefore, our children must be consistently reminded that making rash and ill-informed decisions will only hurt them in the long run. They must take advantage of the wisdom of the men and women who God will place in their lives. For in the abundance of counsel, there is safety.

CHAPTER 12

(Selflessness)

"Look not every man on his own things, but every man also
on the things of others.[5] Let this mind be in you,
which was also in Christ Jesus"
Philippians 2:4-5

It was a cold and dreary Thanksgiving night. The food was looking and smelling good. Turkey, ham, Cornish hens, mac-and-cheese, mashed potatoes, green beans, sweet potato pie and a list of other delicious delicacies graced the table. It seemed as though the entire family was at our house; which was only 1,200 square feet. The laughter, joy, kids playing and love permeated the home. There's nothing like family getting together to share special days, moments and traditions.

As the joyful noise of family and friends permeated our home, I heard a knock at the door. It was a man who we knew as, "Red Hat." We called him, "Red Hat" because he always wore the same old red hat. None of us ever knew his real name. In fact, when I think about it, almost every person I knew in the hood had nicknames. They were called by the nicknames so much, until you literally forgot what their real names were.

Why was "Red Hat" knocking at my door on Thanksgiving Day? You see, Red Hat and I lived in the same neighborhood; and over time we developed a cordial relationship. He would go around the neighborhood knocking on doors to collect returnable bottles and cans. I had tremendous respect for Red Hat because of his gentle spirit, tenacity, and drive to take care of his sister, who was very ill. The only problem that I had with Red Hat was the fact that he would come by my house unexpectedly asking for bottles and cans. To prevent him from coming by my house unexpectedly, I gave him a specific day and approximate time in which to come by. So, every week he would come by to collect the bottles and cans that we saved up for him. That day happened to be Thanksgiving. I informed Red Hat that my family was over and that he would have to come back over the weekend. He complied and proceeded to make his way down the steps and down the street; pushing his cart. While joy and laughter continued to permeate our home, I could not help but think about what had just occurred. It bothered me that I did not welcome Red Hat into my home to dine with my family on Thanksgiving Day. I could not enjoy myself from that point on. I ran down the street and invited him to come and have dinner with us. The look on his face almost brought me to tears. I brought Red Hat into my home and introduced him to the entire family. It was an honor and privilege to have him at the table with my family. And he was seated at the head table. In addition, it was truly a joy to serve him and demonstrate to my entire family what it means to be selfless.

As parents, we must demonstrate to our children what it truly means to be selfless rather than selfish. When all is said and done, the greatness of a man or woman will be determined by what he or she has done to improve the lives of people. This can only be accomplished through servitude. Selflessness doesn't require us to neglect our personal obligations, responsibilities or aspirations. But rather, selflessness demands that we demonstrate the following characteristics:

- Sharing
- Caring
- Serving
- Giving
- Humility
- Understanding
- Listening

There is nothing wrong with being ambitious; but when it drives you to hurt or destroy another person, then that's where the problem comes in. We all struggle with selfishness. It's a part of our sin nature or DNA. In its truest form, sin equates to selfishness. It's all about me, myself and I. In his inaugural address, the late President John F. Kennedy made a renowned proclamation to the American people *"Ask not what your country can do for you, but what you can do for your country."* We must always remember that life does not revolve around our wants and needs, but rather serving and being a blessing to someone else. We must teach our children to have the attitude of sharing, caring, giving, serving and being a blessing to others.

If there was any person that defined what it meant to be "selfless" it was the Lord Jesus Christ. The mind of Christ was one of selflessness as well as sacrifice. He stripped himself of his divinity to become a lowly servant (Philippians 2:1-8). He performed countless miracles, but yet and still he stooped down to wash his disciple's feet. How much more are we to display servitude to our family members, friends and a lost and dying world? When was the last time you engaged in a single act of service, expecting nothing in return? When was the last time you invited a Red Hat into your home to enjoy a meal with your family? When was the last time you served someone beyond the four walls of the church? When was the last time you gave of yourself, your time, talent and treasure in order to be a blessing to someone else?

Right now there may be someone reading this book who hasn't welcome Jesus in your life. Trust me, if you surrender your heart, mind and your entire life to him, he will not let you down. Jesus Christ, the Lord of lords, and King of kings, is standing and knocking at your door; not to collect bottles or cans, but to come in and dine with you; the question is, will you let him in?

Revelation 3:20

Behold, I stand at the door, and knock: if any man hear my voice, and open the door, I will come in to him, and will sup with him, and he with me

T.H.R.E.A.D.S

After 26 years of parenting, coupled with my personal experiences, I strongly believe that these seven principles will aid you in your quest of depositing and developing excellence in your household. I am confident that the THREADS principle will be a blessing to all families regardless of status, ethnicity, religious background or education. If we desire to build strong families, churches, communities and societies as a whole then we must put into practice:

1. *Transparency (speaking the truth in love)*
2. *Honor (teaching and demanding respect, which starts in the home)*
3. *Responsibility (following directions, obeying, accountability, following through)*
4. *Example (teaching them by first being the example)*
5. *Affirmation (encouraging, approving and correcting)*

6. *Decisions (Decisions have consequences. Seek good counsel, learn from past decisions and avoid making decisions under pressure)*
7. *Selflessness (Life does not revolve around you. Be a blessing to someone else)*

(WHERE ARE THEY NOW?)

Rick, Julian, Christian, Jalen and Caleb Sykes

Rick, my oldest son, is still on the road to recovery from the accident. He is doing well, and his legal matters are resolved. Ricky is a gifted musician and serves as the Minister of Music at the Prevailing Church, where yours truly is the pastor. Rick is committed to helping his father build the church and impact the community. He oversees the food distribution program through Forgotten Harvest and assists with managing our Warming Center Project for the homeless during the cold winter months. This dedicated young man is the President/CEO of Y.A.R.D.S (Young Athlete Resources Development and Support). He also has a daughter, Karis Peyton Sykes. Rick, Jr., He is now married to a beautiful and lovely young lady, Alisha. They are expecting their first child.

Julian, is married to the lovely and beautiful, Kamyla. Both of them are committed to mentoring youths. Julian is a gifted musician, songwriter and is the Praise and Worship Leader at the Prevailing Church. Julian desires to play professional basketball overseas and in the process of completing his degree. He is also committed to helping his father grow the church and impact the community by being involved with our youth, the food distribution program and Warming Center Project.

Christian recently graduated from Specs Howard in Digital Media and Graphic Arts. He currently serves as the Director of Graphic Arts and Design. He is also becoming one of the premier bass players in Detroit. Christian desires to travel the world both musically and in the field of missions.

Jalen, is a senior in high school (the class of 2016). He's a 3.3 GPA student and a star athlete on his high school basketball team. Jalen is looking to take his skills to the next level in college and become an Architect. A gifted musician, Jalen also is the drummer at the Prevailing Church. He is also very much involved with our food distribution program and is interested in becoming an architect.

Caleb, is a high school freshman (the class of 2019). He has a 3.0 GPA. He's destined to be a great student-athlete. Caleb serves as the Sound Man and is also a gifted musician at The Prevailing Church. In addition, Caleb is also very much involved with our food distribution program.

I am so grateful that the Lord has blessed my wife and I to have 5 sons committed to serving their community, church, parents and (most importantly) the Lord Jesus Christ. It is my desire that the Lord will continue to prosper and favor these Five Smooth Stones to excel in the gifts, talents and abilities that He has provided them with. Not to be used for selfish reasons, but to be a blessing to all whom they come in contact with.

I am so grateful for my one and only daughter, Kourtney R. Sykes. She is truly a blessing to her family, church and the community. God has granted her with the ability to minister in song. It is my prayer that God will grant her the unique privilege of ministering in song across the world; touching lives. It is also my prayer that she fulfills her purpose in the world and be all that God will have her to be. I want her to know that. I love her, even though sometimes, I know I get on her nerves.

CHAPTER 13

Family Counseling

(A Family That Counsels Together Understands Together)

"Arrogant know-it-alls stir up discord, but wise men and women listen to each other's counsel."
Proverbs 13:10

Who would have ever thought that my entire family needed counseling? If someone would have told me I have to sit in a counseling session (along with my family), I would have never believed it. You see, the aftermath of my oldest son's accident took a tremendous toll on the entire family. Yes, God spared his life, but the road to recovery was extremely exhausting and frustrating for all of us. My son, Rick, was severely injured physically, emotionally, psychologically and yes, mentally. Initially, my wife and I were primarily focused on his physical injuries, which included a broken femur (shattered into 5 pieces, broken pelvis and complete tear of the PCL and ACL; not to mention a scarred hand). Little did we know my son was dealing with an injury that none of us could physically see! If there was one thing that we all knew to be a fact, Rick's personality and demeanor had dramatically changed. He would get angry at the drop of a hat. He couldn't sleep at night and would even pace the floor during the night. He would forget at lot, and his speech was slurred. Rick had this glare in his eyes that said something was going on beyond our comprehension. It was not until someone looked at him and asked me did we ever consult with a psychologist since the accident. I said "No"! The person proceeded to inform me that my son displayed all of the symptoms of someone with a Traumatic Brain Injury (TBI).

During this time, I was blessed me to meet a psychologist by the name of Dr. Deborah Ferguson. She came into our lives at the right moment and at the right time. My wife and I were determined to get the help that our son so desperately needed. So, an appointment was made with Dr. Ferguson, and sure enough, he was diagnosed with TBI. For well over a year, my son had suffered emotionally, psychologically and mentally, and none of us knew it. I was very disappointed with myself because I felt like I had let him down by not knowing and understanding what he was going through internally. Dr. Ferguson informed us that Traumatic Brain Injuries were common for people involved in car accidents. In my son's case, he was t-boned by a semi-truck, which could have been fatal. In order for my son to get better, he would have to attend counseling sessions. Thanks to Dr. Deborah Ferguson and Clyde Alexander for providing the care, love, support and professional attention that my son needed.

There were a few counseling sessions that my wife and I needed to attend. In the first session my wife and I attended, we were overwhelmed, shocked and literally in tears as my son began to share with us what he was going through. We had no idea that he was dealing with depression, regret, anger, hurt, frustration and a deep-seated pain that was beyond both our human comprehension. In the course of this session, I made a statement that I normally would make as a Christian, but especially as a pastor. I said to my son, "Thank God that you are alive!" As innocent as this statement was, it wasn't the right time to make such a statement. I will never forget the counselor's response to my statement. In a nutshell, the counselor kindly said to me, Mr. Sykes, here you have a young man here, who over a year ago, was in excellent shape and condition, playing semi-pro football, could run, jump and the whole nine. Today you have a young man who can barely walk a block without getting tired, and in your son's mind this is not living. He has wrestled with the fact that his life has forever changed. Until he accepts his condition and circumstance, he will not be able to move forward with his life. The counselor's response to my statement was a hard pill to swallow, but I had to swallow my pride and accept the fact that the counselor was right.

The counseling session that the entire family attended was intense, but much more informative. The primary purpose of this counseling session was to inform Rick's brothers and sister about his current condition, and how we must all pull together to support him as he worked through his personal challenges. It was through the family counseling sessions that each one of them understood why Rick's personality and demeanor changed. Upon hearing about their brother's condition, each one of them became more sensitive and understanding towards him from that day forward. All of us made a personal commitment to adjust our normal behavior patterns for the purpose of supporting Rick. For example, anybody who knows the Sykes family, know that we are a very humorous family. Joking and cracking on each other is just a part of the Sykes Family DNA. If you are around long enough, you will discover that having fun is what we do. It's our way of expressing our love for each other.

However, considering the fact that Rick was dealing with so much, we all made a unified commitment to pull back from joking with him. We all noticed that things he would normally laugh about weren't funny anymore. We were all willing to make adjustments, changes, sacrifices and personal commitments to support Rick in any way that we could. I've always been somewhat hard on my son, simply because he was the oldest, but even I had to make adjustments and altar my normal approach when dealing with him. It was very hard, but we were all committed to travel with Rick as he traveled down the road to recovery. In this I learned that Rick's accident was not just about him, but it was also about us as a family. Yes, it is true that *"a family that prays together; stays together."* It is also emphatically true that *"a family that receives counseling together-understands together."* Throughout, this whole ordeal I have come to learn that regardless of your status, education, experience, race, sex, creed or color, all of us need someone that we can share our dreams, desires, and goals. By the same token, we all need someone with whom we can share our hurts, pain and disappointments. Not necessarily just to seek an answer, but more so releasing negative and toxic feelings and thoughts that will eventually get the best of you. We all need someone who will travel with us on the journey of life. Life is truly a journey, and all who seek to travel alone (will for the most part) succumb to the challenges and disappointments associated with it. Attending the various counseling sessions along with my family allowed me to not only better understand my son, but also yours truly. Recently, I shared with my son that think I need to see a counselor because I think I haven't gotten over everything associated with the accidents, including almost losing him. I think I'm going to do it!

A very special thanks to all of the wonderful professionals who assisted my son, Rick and the family, through one of the toughest periods of our lives. Thanks, Ms. Kelly MacAulay

(Case Manager), Ms. Sue Rice (Case Manager), Dr. Robert Ferguson, MD (Gastroenterologist/Internal Medicine), Dr. Richard Klein (DDS/TMJ), Dr. Jerome Branham (DDS), Attorney Heather Atnip, Attorney David Gorosh and the law offices of Geoffrey Fieger.

Message For Single Mothers

For all of those single mothers and grandparents who have taken on the tremendous challenge and responsibility of raising children, I salute you. I realize that it can be difficult dealing with the struggles associated with parenting; especially when you're doing it all by yourself. As I stated earlier, my mom was a single parent. And so, I am familiar with the struggles that single mothers have to endure when raising children, especially males. I understand what grandmothers go through with raising their grandchildren, because I saw my grandmother do it.

The task of raising children (even within a two-parent home) is tedious and exhausting. But remember that the way you handle the entire situation will, for the most part, determine the outcome. There is a universal law in the Bible that applies to all mankind regardless of race, religion, gender, status or education. And that universal law simply says, "Whatsoever a man plants, that shall he also reap." (Gal.6:7). You nor I can change the consequences of our past. But what we can do is start afresh by planting seeds into good soil; expecting a good harvest in return. There are several things that you can do that will enable you to deposit and develop your sons and daughters to become emotionally, mentally and even spiritually healthy. Diligently following these seven rules that I have laid out will aid you as you navigate through this journey of single parenting.

Rule #1:
Never talk negatively to (or in front) of your child/or children about their father. This is a major mistake and could prove costly in the long-run.

Rule #2:
Spend your time and energy on the well-being of your children (education, health, family, character building, etc.)

Rule #3:
Seek counsel and get assistance from other resources, such as mentorship program, activities, volunteering and other productive outlets. You can't do this by yourself!

Rule #4:
Learn to listen to your children. Strive to build a two-way relationship rather than a one-way. This can only be accomplished if we as, parents, learn to listen with our hearts rather than our heads.

Rule #5:
Don't ever compare your children to each other. Showing favoritism can be devastating to a child.

Rule #6:
Don't talk down to your children. Constructive criticism is good, but make sure you choose your words carefully. Remember that they are people, too.

Rule #7:
Never allow your anger, resentment or frustration that you have towards the father transmit to the child (or children). They're not responsible for being here!

(Ackowledgments)

"Mark the perfect man, and behold the upright:
for the end of that man is peace"
Psalms 37:37

I am grateful for the men who God placed in my life in order to fill those gaps that were missing. I would love to tell you that I became the man that I am on my own; but that would be farthest from the truth. Therefore, I would like to honor all of the men who were instrumental in shaping this stone (myself) who was once riddled with dents, rough edges, holes and in dry places. Two words to describe the following men:

The late Robert Dandridge (my grandfather)
(hard work and discipline)
The late Pastor James M. Maclin, Sr.
(prayer and no-nonsense)
Pastor Alan R. Evans, I (charisma and family man)

Bishop Phillip A. Brooks (loyalty and dedication)
The late Pastor Lorris Upshaw, Sr.
(generosity and strength)
Bishop Ben Gibert (excellence and vision)
The late Bishop Willie Harris (love and integrity)
Pastor Ernie McCutchen (quietness and sincerity)
The late Elder Calvin Gunn (intelligence and authenticity)
Sylvester Johnson, my father-in-law
(acceptance and affirmation)
Pastor Terrell Humes (teacher, encourager)
Pastor Anthony Humes (teacher, encourager)
Elder Eddie Blaine (listener, challenger)
Mr. Charles Ross (mentor, friend)

CPSIA information can be obtained
at www.ICGtesting.com
Printed in the USA
FSOW02n0601271116
27770FS

9 781498 456227